INTRO TO
SHOW JUMPING

BY SARAH ASWELL

SADDLE UP!

SportsZone

An Imprint of Abdo Publishing
abdopublishing.com

Handwritten: 798.2 5

abdopublishing.com

Published by Abdo Publishing, a division of ABDO, PO Box 398166, Minneapolis, Minnesota 55439. Copyright © 2018 by Abdo Consulting Group, Inc. International copyrights reserved in all countries. No part of this book may be reproduced in any form without written permission from the publisher. SportsZone™ is a trademark and logo of Abdo Publishing.

Printed in the United States of America, North Mankato, Minnesota
092017
012018

Cover Photo: Abramova Kseniya/iStockphoto
Interior Photos: Abramova Kseniya/iStockphoto, 1; George Silk/The LIFE Picture Collection/Getty Images, 5, 6–7; Michael Gamble/Alamy, 9; Eddy Lemaistre/KMSP/DPPI/Icon Sportswire, 10–11; Pascal Muller/EQ Images/Icon Sportswire, 13; The Print Collector/Hulton Archive/Getty Images, 15; De Agostini Picture Library/DeAgostini/Getty Images, 16–17; NCJ - Topix/Mirrorpix/Newscom, 19; DB/picture-alliance/dpa/AP Images, 21; Anastasija Popova/Shutterstock Images, 23, 34; Greg Balfour Evans/Alamy, 24–25; iStockphoto, 28–29, 45; Cao haigen/Imaginechina/AP Images, 30; Rob Griffith/AP Images, 33; NurPhoto/Getty Images, 37; Michel Euler/AP Images, 39; Shutterstock Images, 41; Julie Badrick/Alamy, 42

Editor: Marie Pearson
Series Designer: Laura Polzin
Content Consultant: Paige Clark, B.S. Equine Science, University of Minnesota Crookston

Publisher's Cataloging-in-Publication Data
Names: Aswell, Sarah, author.
Title: Intro to show jumping / by Sarah Aswell.
Description: Minneapolis, Minnesota : Abdo Publishing, 2018. | Series: Saddle up! | Includes online resources and index.
Identifiers: LCCN 2017946882 | ISBN 9781532113444 (lib.bdg.) | ISBN 9781532152320 (ebook)
Subjects: LCSH: Show Jumping--Juvenile literature. | Jumping (Horsemanship)--Juvenile literature. | Horse sports--Juvenile literature.
Classification: DDC 798.25--dc23
LC record available at https://lccn.loc.gov/2017946882

TABLE OF
CONTENTS

CHAPTER 1
THE SKILLS AND THRILLS OF SHOW JUMPING 4

CHAPTER 2
THE HISTORY OF SHOW JUMPING 14

CHAPTER 3
RULES AND REGULATIONS 22

CHAPTER 4
TRAINING, EQUIPMENT, AND ATTIRE 32

CHAPTER 5
COMPETITIONS: WHAT TO EXPECT 40

GLOSSARY 46

ONLINE RESOURCES................................. 47

MORE INFORMATION 47

INDEX.. 48

ABOUT THE AUTHOR 48

1

THE SKILLS AND THRILLS OF SHOW JUMPING

In 1956, a man named Harry de Leyer went to a horse auction. He saw a dirty, skinny plow horse headed to the slaughterhouse and felt a connection to the animal. De Leyer saved the horse by buying him for just $80. De Leyer named the horse Snowman and sold him. But the horse kept escaping and returning to de Leyer's farm. To get there, he had to jump many tall fences. De Leyer then

De Leyer originally bought Snowman to use as a children's school horse before he sold him.

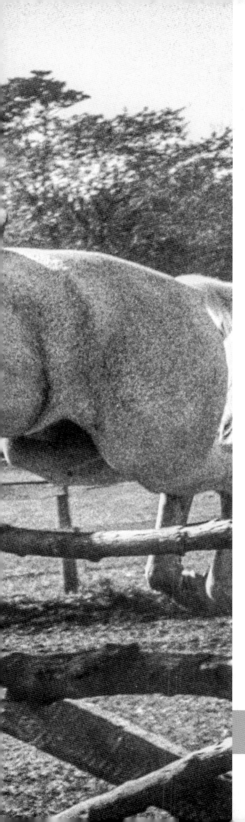

knew the horse was very special and bought the horse back. He trained him to show jump.

Just two years later, Snowman was a famous show jumper. He won the Open Jumper Championship at Madison Square Garden's Diamond Jubilee two years in a row, and the United States Equestrian Federation named him Horse of the Year.

Snowman's story illustrates that any type of horse can be trained to show jump, not just purebred horses. In the end, show jumping is about the horse and its rider working together to succeed.

Snowman became a great show jumper.

WHAT IS SHOW JUMPING?

Show jumping is a team and individual Olympic equestrian sport. In show jumping, a rider guides a horse through a series of jumps. They must move quickly through the course, careful not to miss jumps, knock down barriers, or fall down. The team that makes the fewest mistakes in the fastest time wins.

Show jumping is a fast, exciting, and colorful event. It's both thrilling to participate in and thrilling to watch. Spectators sit in a stadium to watch the action as each horse takes its turn running the course. The course usually features between 10 and 15 jumping obstacles. Each obstacle is different. One jump might be a low fence with a pool of water in front of it. Another jump might be a high wall. Some jumps may be very close together, while others are far apart. The obstacles are often brightly painted and decorated.

Riders compete either as individuals or as teams. Male and female riders compete together. In small contests, riders may compete for a ribbon or trophy. In large contests, riders compete for prize money along with trophies or medals.

SHOW JUMPING HORSES

The best show jumping horses are strong and agile. Many are tall with long legs and have long necks for balance. Most have a flat, broad saddle area so that the rider is secure. Most have good lungs, which help the horse take big breaths and finish the course faster. All show jumpers

Show jumping arenas have a variety of colorful jumps.

The French equestrian team took gold in the 2016 Rio Olympics with one stallion, one gelding, and two mares.

need to be strong to jump and absorb the impact upon landing. The personality of a jumper is very important. A brave, careful, and focused horse will excel in the arena. A good temperament is vital in addition to the horse's physical talents and health. The gender of the horse does not matter. Mares, stallions, and geldings have all won major competitions in recent years.

SHOW JUMPING BREEDS

At lower levels, horses and ponies of a wide range of breeds and sizes compete in show jumping. At beginner and junior levels, a horse or pony must simply be healthy and strong with good manners and confidence to begin training.

As the competition gets tougher and the jumps get higher, riders may use certain types of horses that tend to perform better. Today, most jumping horses are warmbloods, horses often bred for equestrian sports such as dressage and show jumping. The most popular breeds of warmbloods for jumping are Dutch warmbloods, Belgian warmbloods, and Selle Français. But any horse may still compete.

WHAT MAKES A GREAT SHOW JUMPING HORSE?

A great show jumping horse must be athletic, healthy, and free of injury, with good show jumping structure. The horse must have lots of careful training and be confident and not fearful. The horse must also have a great relationship with its rider.

Warmbloods swept the podium in the 2016 Summer Olympics individual show jumping event. The winner was Big Star, a 14-year-old Dutch warmblood stallion. The silver medal winner was All In, a 10-year-old Dutch warmblood gelding. The bronze medal winner was Fine Lady 5, a 13-year-old Hanoverian mare.

Big Star, ridden by Nick Skelton, clears a jump at the 2016 Olympics.

2

THE HISTORY OF SHOW JUMPING

As long as people have ridden horses, they have needed to clear obstacles such as logs and ditches. But the sport of show jumping did not develop until the 1700s. At this time, a British law called the Enclosure Act required landowners to build fences around their property. Because of the fences, foxhunters could no longer follow their dogs without a horse that could jump fences. Soon, jump training became popular. Leaping contests began around 1850. Horses would jump over a single hedge or fence. The horse that jumped the highest won.

During foxhunts, horses needed to clear fences, walls, and hedges.

THE FATHER OF MODERN JUMPING

Captain Federico Caprilli was born in Italy in 1868. He was a teacher for the Italian Cavalry. Caprilli watched horses jump without riders. He discovered that riders should lean forward, not backward, when jumping. Leaning forward doesn't weigh the back of the horse down and makes it easier for the horse to balance.

He also shortened the saddle's stirrups, so that the rider could lift his or her seat out of the saddle during jumps. This gave the horse more balance and kept the rider's weight from hurting the horse's back. Finally, he taught riders not to

Caprilli, on the horse Pouf, demonstrates how to lean forward for a jump.

interfere with the horse's natural ability to jump. He didn't want the rider to completely control the horse. He wanted the horse and rider to be a team. The Caprilli technique spread across Italy and the world. Riders still use it today.

MAKING THE SPORT

Show jumping became an official Olympic sport in 1912. For 40 years, only military officers could compete in the sport. But when horses were no longer regularly used in war, civilian riders entered the spotlight. Show jumping became much more popular in the 1950s when it was televised. The decorated courses and dramatic jumps were fun for everyone—even those who didn't know much about the sport—to watch.

Women were first allowed to compete in the show jumping event in the 1956 Olympics, and they have been a part of the sport ever since. Women and men compete against each other in show jumping. Marion Mould was the first woman to win an individual show jumping medal in the Olympics. She won a silver medal in 1968 in Mexico

Mould (competing as Marion Coakes before she married) jumps a pool on Stroller in 1965.

City with her extraordinary pony, Stroller. Stroller was a small 14.2-hand pony that did not look like a show jumper. But Mould believed in him. They won competitions across England before shocking the world by placing second in the 1968 Mexico City Olympics. Mould was just 18 years old.

HISTORIC HORSES

Show jumping takes amazing athletic ability as well as heart. In the last 150 years, many special horses have captured international attention. Snowman, the former plow horse, defied all odds to become Horse of the Year in 1958. Known for his calm nature and hard work, Snowman was inducted into the United States Show Jumping Hall of Fame in 1992.

Halla was a Standardbred mare that was difficult to train. But when she was paired with German rider Hans Günter Winkler in 1951, the team was

A LEGENDARY TEAM

Hans Günter Winkler is the only rider to win five Olympic show jumping medals. His horse Halla is the only horse to win three Olympic gold medals.

Winkler and Halla at the 1956 Stockholm Olympics.

unstoppable. Halla and Winkler both hold records for the most Olympic gold medals won in show jumping. Halla won 125 competitions during her career.

3

RULES AND REGULATIONS

Show jumping tests the skills of both the horse and rider. A horse must be fast, strong, and brave. The rider must be smart, precise, athletic, and skilled. Together, they have to try to navigate the course without making mistakes before time runs out.

THE COURSE AND ARENA

The arena is a large circular area surrounded by stands or a stadium. Arenas can be indoors or outdoors. Most are approximately 200 feet by 100 feet (61 m by 31 m) in size.

Show jumping takes focus and skill.

The arena should be firm enough to support the horse's takeoff and landing, but also slightly springy to absorb the impact of landing.

The course is made up of a series of obstacles that must be jumped in a certain order. The obstacles are set up to test the horse and rider's skill at jumping and turning.

A course designer makes and decorates the course. All courses are different.

BEFORE THE COMPETITION

Before the show starts, teams are not allowed to practice on the course. However, riders are encouraged to walk the course. While walking the course, riders figure out how sharp or wide to take a turn. Riders also measure the distance between jumps to figure out how many strides their horse will take. They do this by counting their strides. Two human strides equal the distance of a horse's takeoff and landing. Four human strides equal the distance of approximately one canter stride of a horse.

Horses and riders are allowed to warm up in the paddock or schooling area, a small arena that usually has a couple of jumps. The judges draw names randomly

WALKING A COURSE

Riders look at several things when walking a course. They look at the entire course from the horse's point of view, noting possible distractions. They also note the footing of the ground. When finished, they stand in the middle of the course and mentally ride it.

to determine jumping order for the first round. The next rounds are jumped from lowest score to highest.

THE JUMPS

There are many types of jumps. Jumps can be high, low, narrow, or wide. Some may be sloped, while others may have a pool of water, called a Liverpool. Many jumps are made of railed fences, but others look like walls. All fences are designed so that a horse and rider won't get hurt even if they don't clear the jump. Safety cups hold the fence rails up. But the rails can fall down if a horse hits them.

Some common jumps include verticals, which are high fences with two or more rails placed on top of one another. Oxers are jumps that combine two verticals to create a wider obstacle. Triple bars are three vertical fences placed together, with a low bar in front and the next two bars behind it placed increasingly higher. Combinations are when two or three jumps are placed just one or two strides apart.

Each jump is numbered and has a red flag on its right side and a white flag on its left side. The course designer often decorates the jumps. A jump may have bright colors, flower boxes, plants, or gates. Jump decorations make the sport more exciting to watch and test the horse's willingness to take unfamiliar jumps.

SCORING

Show jumping judges score horses and riders by counting their mistakes. Different types of mistakes result in a different number of faults. In most competitions, knocking down a pole or stepping in water counts for four faults. Refusing to make a jump counts for four faults, while a second or third refusal can result in elimination. If the horse or rider falls, they can be eliminated.

The red flag needs to be to the right and the white flag to the left of the horse and rider when they jump.

Beginner show jumping contests allow more mistakes before elimination.

The course must be completed in a certain amount of time, usually in approximately 75 seconds. For every second over time allowed, one fault is added to the pair's score. The team with the fewest faults wins.

If a horse and rider don't get any faults, they "go clear." If more than one team goes clear or if there is a tie, there is a tiebreaker known as a jump-off. A jump-off takes place on a shorter but harder course. The jumps may be higher, and there may be tough combination jumps. The horse that goes clear wins. If more than one horse goes clear, the fastest horse wins.

Jump-off fences can be very high.

4

TRAINING, EQUIPMENT, AND ATTIRE

Show jumping requires a lot of hard work and training for rider and horse. It also requires proper equipment for the horse and proper attire for the rider. Show jumping is a difficult feat that requires great skill and lots of practice. A jump has five phases: approach, takeoff, flight, landing, and departure.

Riders need to focus on the current jump as well as plan their path to the next jump while riding a course.

As a rider approaches a jump, the rider needs to control the direction of the horse so that the horse jumps at the right angle. Next, the rider must maintain the horse's speed so the team can clear the jump safely and finish the course quickly. At the same time, the rider must time the horse's stride so that it takes off from the right spot. Finally, the rider must keep his or her balance so that neither the horse nor the rider falls during takeoff or landing. Riders and horses must be calm and confident. A fearful horse or rider can cause a refusal.

LEARNING TO JUMP

A horse learns to jump first by going over one or two poles lying on the ground. The poles are then replaced by two low cross rails raised off the ground, and then by a low vertical rail. At first, a trainer may need to remain on the ground and guide the horse by a long rein. When jumping, riders should allow the horse to jump naturally while also safely controlling the horse.

Ground poles are also used to teach beginning show jumpers.

Beginning riders need to practice jumping position. In jumping position, a rider rises out of the saddle. The rider should balance with his or her feet in the stirrups, looking ahead.

RIDER GEAR

All show jumping clothes should be comfortable and allow the rider to move freely. Riders need riding helmets to protect against falls, gloves to help grip the reins, and a show jumping coat worn over a collared shirt and tie. They also need riding breeches and field boots with laces, nonslip soles, and flexible ankles. Some riders carry a crop, though it is not often used. Professional riders often wear spurs as a jumping aid. But these spurs should not be sharp enough to harm the horse.

HORSE EQUIPMENT

A horse's show jumping equipment either aids it in jumping or protects it from injury. Horses wear a special saddle with a shallow seat. That and short stirrups help the rider rise out of the saddle for a jump. The reins,

Gloves help riders grip the reins.

HORSESHOE STUDS

Studs are used for a horse's hooves, giving them better grip during takeoffs. Sharp studs are used for hard or slippery surfaces, while fat studs are used in muddy conditions. When a horse is not jumping, flat studs or stud fillers are used on pavement to keep the stud holes protected.

bridle, and bit allow the rider to control the horse throughout the course.

Horseshoes protect the horse's feet. Horseshoe studs are screwed onto each shoe to improve the foot's grip. Horse boots protect the horse's tendons and heels from injury. Most horses wear overreach boots, foreleg boots, and fetlock boots. A belly guard protects the horse from the studs in its foreleg horseshoes. Many horses also wear a martingale, which keeps the horse's head from coming up too high.

SHOW JUMPING
GEAR

HELMET

COAT

GLOVES

BREECHES

BREASTPLATE

JUMPING SADDLE

FIELD BOOTS

BOOTS

BELLY GUARD

MARTINGALE

5

COMPETITIONS: WHAT TO EXPECT

Show jumping competitions exist for all levels of horse and rider. There are a large number of show jumping classes, events, and levels around the world. The United States has levels 0 to 9 in jumping competitions. Each level has a maximum fence height, a maximum fence width, and a maximum Liverpool length. Level 0 has a maximum fence height of 35 inches (88.9 cm). Level 9 has a maximum fence height of 5 feet (1.5 m).

TYPES OF EVENTS

The Grand Prix is the highest level of show jumping competition. It is run under Fédération Équestre Internationale (FEI) rules. Grand Prix competitions include the Olympics, the World Equestrian Games, the World Cup Series, and the Nations Cup Series.

Puissance is a high jump competition. In French, *puissance* means "strength." Most puissance competitions involve just one jump, which becomes higher after each round. By the end of the competition, the wall may be higher than 7 feet (2.1 m) tall. The record for the highest jump was 8 feet 1 inch (2.47 m). In many puissance competitions, the obstacle is a wall made of bright red "bricks," which are made of plastic

SHOW JUMPING ASSOCIATIONS AROUND THE WORLD

Some popular show jumping associations include the FEI and United States Equestrian Federation. The British Show Jumping Association, the United States Pony Club, and the Western Australian Show Jumping Association are also well known.

The horse and rider make daring vertical leaps in puissance.

or plywood and felt so the horse does not get hurt. The jump can also include poles. After each round, a new layer of bricks is added to the top.

Show jumping is also one of the phases in eventing. Eventing tests horses and riders on dressage, cross-country, and show jumping. Dressage is a sport that shows how well a horse can follow instructions and make intricate movements in an open arena. Dressage requires lots of training, precision, and discipline. Cross-country involves riding up to 4 miles (6.4 km) over 24 to 36 obstacles. Cross-country races require stamina, bravery, and strength. The final test is show jumping. How well a team performs across all three events determines how they place.

HAVING A GREAT COMPETITION DAY

It's normal for both horse and rider to be nervous on competition day. Spectators fill the stands, and there are many sights and sounds. If the rider stays calm, this will help the horse stay calm and improve the performance. A nervous rider will lead to a nervous horse.

Whether practicing or competing, it's important to remember to have fun.

Riders can succeed on competition day by remembering their training, focusing on the course, and setting goals for the day. They can warm up in the paddock and groom their horses to prepare and relax. Most of all, riders should remember to enjoy themselves. They have trained hard to learn jumping with a special horse, and now it is time to show the world what they can do.

GLOSSARY

BREECHES
Snug-fitting riding pants.

CAVALRY
A former division of the military involving soldiers on horseback.

CIVILIAN
People who are not part of the military.

CROP
A short riding whip.

CROSS RAILS
A jump made of two rails that cross to form an x.

EQUESTRIAN
Related to horses.

FOOTING
The condition of the ground beneath the horse.

FORELEG
The front leg of an animal.

GELDING
A male horse that has been surgically made unable to reproduce.

MARE
A female horse.

OBSTACLE
Something that blocks the way and must be overcome to proceed.

PADDOCK
A fenced area for exercising horses.

STALLION
A male horse that is able to reproduce.

STIRRUP
A ring that hangs from a horse's saddle used to hold a rider's foot.

ONLINE RESOURCES

Booklinks
NONFICTION NETWORK
FREE! ONLINE NONFICTION RESOURCES

To learn more about show jumping, visit **abdobooklinks.com**. These links are routinely monitored and updated to provide the most current information available.

MORE INFORMATION

BOOKS

Harris, Susan E. *The United States Pony Club Manual of Horsemanship: Basics for Beginners/D Level*. Hoboken, NJ: Wiley, 2012.

Sanderson, Whitney. *Dressage*. Minneapolis, MN: Abdo Publishing, 2018.

Sanderson, Whitney. *Eventing*. Minneapolis, MN: Abdo Publishing, 2018.

INDEX

British Show Jumping Association, 43

Caprilli, Federico, 17–18
competitions, 8, 10–11, 18–21, 26–31, 40, 43–45

de Leyer, Harry, 4

Enclosure Act, 14
eventing, 44

Fédération Équestre Internationale (FEI), 43

gear, 36, 38, 39

Halla, 20–21
history, 14, 17–18, 20–21

military, 18
Mould, Marion, 18, 20

obstacles, 8, 25, 27–28, 35, 43, 44
Olympic Games, 8, 12, 18–21, 43

puissance, 43–44

scoring, 28, 31
skills, 22, 25, 35
Snowman, 4, 7, 20
Stroller, 20

training, 7, 11, 14, 32, 35–36, 44, 45
types of horses, 9–12

United States Equestrian Federation, 7, 43
United States Pony Club, 43

walking the course, 26
warm up, 26, 45
Western Australian Show Jumping Association, 43
Winkler, Hans Günter, 20–21
women, 18

ABOUT THE AUTHOR

Sarah Aswell is a writer who lives in Missoula, Montana. Her husband is a sports writer. They have two daughters and a dog named Stringer.